1

The First People drew many things.

3

What were these things?

5

These were special spirit people.

7

These spirit people made all
things.

© Knowledge Books and Software

This was God to the First People.

**11**

There were other powerful
beings.

**12**

**13**

Some were big animals that lived on the land.

**15**

What was this creature that
made the land?

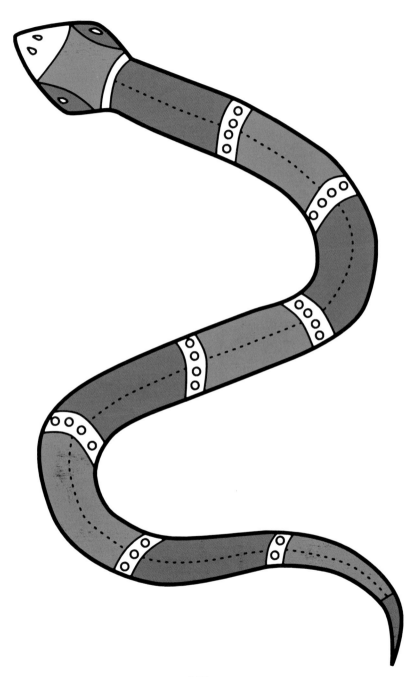

17

Many First Peoples talked of a giant snake.

The rainbow snake laid across the land.

21

The snake formed the rivers and mountains.

# Word bank

people

drew

things

special

spirit

powerful

beings

animals

lived

creature

giant

across

mountains

rivers